Destined My Cash

Are You Destined to Become Wealthy? Your Journey To Your Financial Freedom.

David A. Alcala

Table Of Content

Chapter 1

Are Certain Individuals Bound To Become Rich While Others Aren't?

Not as in ordained by the stars, but rather yes as predetermined by the karma of who their folks are. Well-off people groups' youngsters are naturally given open doors that working-class and lower-class people groups' kids are not.

There is the saying "It's not what you know yet who you know" that applies to this accurate circumstance. If you are attempting to raise capital for a business, experiencing childhood in a well-off circle might make that a lot more straightforward, than having

experienced childhood in an unfortunate cycle. Affluent individuals will generally have more cash to contribute and face the challenge while needy individuals burn through the greater part of their pay to simply make due.
How rich would you like to be?

Recently, I was working at my Thai café.
A young lady came in late around evening time to get her to-go request.
She said, "I requested on Grubhub, yet could I at any point leave a tip for you all with my charge card?"

We illuminated her, "No, apologies. You'd need to purchase something and sign a receipt to tip us."
The young lady then, at that point, requested a mixed drink to go.
She left a $100 tip on a $10 tab.

I might want to be simply rich.

Indeed, there is a great deal of truth to that. A few elements go into it like training, pay, and how they oversee cash. By and large, assuming you have training in the right regions you will get more cash flow than in different regions. Pay is unquestionably a major component yet certain individuals rake in some serious cash yet don't have any idea how to oversee cash and hence have genuinely low total assets. Then again, some Individuals don't get a lot of cash flow yet figure out how to live on short of what they make and contribute the rest of over an extensive period, in some cases a long period of 30 or 40 years, and have extremely high total assets.

What prevents everybody from becoming rich?

I've been poor as damnation and I've been rich.

I can perceive you that who I was the point at which I was destitute was WAY not quite the same as who I'm today as a rich business visionary.

Here are only a couple of the reasons I was destitute previously (and the primary reasons that most others are poor).

1. *Squirrels!*

Have you at any point seen the film 'Up'?

Do you recall the brilliant retriever Doug who might consistently get diverted mid-sentence by an out-of-control squirrel?

The main explanation is that a great many people stay broke.

A great many people bounce from one business to another, profession to vocation, thought to thought never adhering to ONE thing until it's productive.
Throughout recent years, I've been enticed by Each industry in the world.

Yet, I stayed with my ONE money manager (training/self-improvement) and, subsequently, have made millions with it.
Listen to this...
You CAN get rich with pretty much any business or commission-based vocation.
However, you need to stay with it for quite a while before you'll bring in the cash you need.
To get rich, screw glossy article condition. Try out another plan of action consistently for a very long time. Toward the finish of the half year, pick the ONE plan of action you

partook in the most and stay with that for the following 5 years.

Assuming you attempt to get 1% better at that business regularly, you will be rich in 60 months.

2. *They Have Terrible Sensitivities*

The second explanation that the vast majority won't ever be rich is that they have terrible sensitivities.

I'm not discussing nuts or sensitivities to pollen.

I imply that they are "hypersensitive" to difficult work and discipline.

The simple idea of getting up right on time, perusing as opposed to staring at the television, and giving an additional 3 hours every day to their second job makes them seem to be this...

I'll simply be genuine with you...

A great many people don't have the stuff to be rich.
They assume they need riches, yet what they truly need is to get higher than Sneak Home slice and sit on the sofa gorging Netflix.

Getting rich requires penance. It is not necessarily the case that you can't have a great time while you get rich. In any case, you should surrender things you love, do things you would rather not do, and persevere through a decent measure of torment and vulnerability.
So deal with it or get out.
I couldn't care less if you're too apathetic to be in any way rich. That is cool. You do you.

Yet, don't bitch and groan about how uncalled for it is that others are making 6, 7, and 8 figures when you're not in any event, able to put down the damn television remote and get a book.

3. *They Revere Beavis*

Have you at any point seen the Television program Beavis and Butthead?
If you have, you could know where I'm going with this...
Quite possibly the Main motivation that individuals won't ever get rich is because they invest all of their energy with buttheads.

Here's the way things are looking.
Assuming you invest energy with broke despondent individuals, that is everything you'll at any point be.
I realize that you love your companions.
It all makes sense to me, I truly do.
Furthermore, it is not necessarily the case

that you can't invest energy with individuals who aren't rich to become well off.

Be that as it may, you Can't invest your energy with harmful, pessimistic, destitution disapproved of individuals and hope to bring in any genuine cash.
Encircle yourself with affluent, cheerful, and fruitful individuals and you'll begin to take on their propensities.
Encircle yourself with dolts and you'll embrace theirs.
Need to be rich? Quit spending time with buttheads.

4. They're Goodey Two Shoes

Alright, so this one could take some making sense of.

I'd contend that quite possibly the main motivation individuals never become rich is because they're as well "great".

In other words, they attempt and do everything right and observe the guidelines that their families, companions, and society have spread out for them.
News streak! You Won't ever get rich by keeping the guidelines.

You needn't bother with being exploitative or doing anything unlawful.
In any case, assuming that you get involved with the b.s. that you ought to head off to college, find a decent line of work, and move gradually up the stepping stool... You're in a bad way.

Beyond essential morals and cultural standards (you know, such as wearing your

clothing within your jeans) there are NO principles with regards to bringing in cash.
You can get rich quickly (yet difficult). You can get rich without a degree. You can get rich without representatives. You can get rich without having an item to sell.
Figure out how and when you break the Brules (horse crap rules) and your lucrative endeavors will speed up dramatically.

5. They're Offbeat

Whenever I hear somebody utter the expression, "You're not kidding", my stomach response is to strike the poop out of them and afterward shout at them like a coked-up military trainer.

That is not what I do (you know... since jail sucks), yet that is the way it causes me to feel.

Stop and think for a minute...

Karma IS significant. There's a specific level of "karma" and fortune at play concerning creating FU's financial well-being.

Yet, you can make your karma by teaching yourself, really buckling down, and placing yourself in the right circumstances.

Assuming you accept the promotion that rich individuals are fortunate or that you can't become rich because the universe has it out for you... You're in a bad way.

For what reason mightn't I at any point be rich, what am I fouling up that rich individuals are doing well?

The inquiry you ought to present is how might I be rich, not the opposite way around. If you inquire as to for what reason mightn't at any point be rich, then your cerebrum, your sub-awareness will proceed to look for every one of the justifications for what reason you're not rich. If you ask positively, your psyche will give its all to figure out how to make you rich. It's how you approach life overall. Attempting and cutting out the negatives in your day-to-day existence will assist you with going far to arrive at your objectives.

What's holding you back from being rich?
Nothing. I became rich by putting resources into the land beginning
At the point when I was 21. I drove a bad vehicle, didn't have extravagant garments or costly toys, didn't eat at costly cafés or hang out at bars, and so on. My companions chuckled at my way of life. At 39 I had procured nine houses, an apartment

complex, and enormous plots of lacking area. I resigned to Hawaii and my companions quit chuckling.

For what reason are there such countless needy individuals in this world?
They're not.
They work for it or have conditions that give it.
There is no predetermination.
I need to be well off and effective however I don't have any idea where to begin. Where do I start?
The best way to become well off is by utilizing business influence to bring you benefits.

Chapter 2

Business influence:

1. Utilize others' time (Workers)
2. Utilize others' cash (Supporting)
3. Utilization of innovations (Mechanical technology, PCs, hardware, this region is gigantic.)
4. Utilization of Intelectual Properties (Licenses, brand names, copyrights)

Main concern:

Never at any point trade your time for cash - that has zero influence and will diminish your opportunities to accomplish your desired material objectives...

How might I become rich?

Sell tea.

As indicated by Marwari's rationale,

If you sell a solitary cup of tea:
Creation cost = ₹ 3, Selling cost= ₹ 10, Profit= ₹ 7
If 500 cups of tea are sold in a day:
Benefit in a day = Three thousand and 500 rupees.
Benefit in a month = One lakh and 5,000 rupees.
Benefit in a year = Twelve lakh and 60,000 rupees.
In this way, now is the right time to move that degree and say, "Chai, chai." (tea, hot tea.)

For what reason do a few rich individuals suppose they aren't rich?
I have various companions that are very well off to staggeringly affluent. Some are strangely rich.

At the point when I'm with my companions, I'm frequently among the least fortunate in the room.

Maybe the explanation a few rich individuals don't see themselves as well off is that they know so many others that are a ton richer than they are.

My folks are poor. How would I become rich without trying sincerely or acquiring somebody's resources?

All things considered, let me see your inquiry, Do you need to become rich without trying sincerely or acquiring someone's resources? Alright let me let you know what you can do

first, go to your bed

second, sleep

the third dream is that you become rich without sitting idle and fourth last step, you are rich now, however just in your fantasy, simply trust you won't ever awaken from this point onward so you will continuously be rich.

For what reason don't I feel rich when I make $2,000 benefit/day? A great many people don't make that in a month.
This feels like either an unfortunate endeavor at a humblebrag, or a surprisingly more dreadful endeavor to snare individuals into anything fraudulent business model you're wanting to benefit from. Might you at any point explain which it is?

For what reason aren't more individuals becoming well-off?
They don't understand that they can be. Thus, they don't for a moment even attempt. It's all in our outlook. Commonly I see that somebody is following through with

something and it occurs to me that I can do likewise: be an expert, begin a business, and venture to the far corners of the planet. 90% of achievement is appearing. A great many people won't ever make an appearance.

For what reason isn't everybody rich and fruitful?
Two reasons:
1. Since they don't have a clue about their value.
2. They would rather not know.

They don't have cash since they would rather not confront their apprehension or battle the apathy to sort out the amount they're worth.
The human mind is the most impressive thing on the planet. Crap, it's essentially obliterating Earth due to its power.

Be that as it may, individuals underselling themselves is the thing I'm attempting to get at.

They'd prefer to stay at a particular employment that pays them for their time since they're too terrified to go out and get compensated for what they're worth.

All fruitful individuals grasp this.

For what reason in all actuality do individuals not regard me?

Might it be said that you are excessively guiltless and legitimate? then it works out. Since the world is poop today and they don't like individuals with genuineness and reliability.

I'm 18, and all I care about is turning out to be very rich, why would that be? I'll

I would call you a normal high schooler.

The fact of the matter is generally a couple of adolescents (or adults...) have a specific energy. The modest bunch of individuals that foster some ability in artistic expression frequently utilize that to be more appealing to other people...

Your choice to drink bourbon won't work well for you. On the off chance that you have no control over that all alone, get help pronto.
Stupidly accepting that wealth is either conceivable or an answer for your absence of associations with real wellsprings of fulfillment will comparably not serve you well.

Assuming you foster abilities that will empower you to find true success you have some kind of possibility of basically having real achievement.

Do the rich believe that others should become rich?

Many individuals like me need to see many individuals ascending all alone.
I answered about abundance and it's for the ones who need assistance.
Many out there will see a ton of fascinating and imaginative individuals ascending.
Well, the main motivation for most who are as yet unchanged before 20 years is that they don't need to be rich. Most need a task and a house which piss me out.

Just the visionaries and practitioners can achieve their ideal objectives before death.
I'm an independent man I have even cleaned latrines and picked up trash a long time back.

In any case, things have changed and today I visit those spots in my fantasy vehicles and ponder how it was and the way that I emerged from the working class futile way of life.

I recall once working at a cheap food corner.
I had a companion whom I told I'm need to be rich and I need to satisfy my fantasies.
He answered its beyond the realm of possibilities for destitute individuals like us.
We will wind up working here until the end of time.
Well, he hadn't had large dreams. after 2 years I was making 7 figures and he was still there.

A great many people are exceptionally pessimistic so they beat down themselves.

Well on the off chance that anybody needs any assistance feel with liberating to utilize Quora informing.
Not cash and gifts but rather pieces of advice.

Could an uninformed individual at any point become rich?
Totally!

I know a man with 6th-grade schooling that was down to his last $200. He was up late one evening agonizing over how he planned to deal with his young family. He was functioning as a Volkswagen car technician, yet had quite recently lost his employment since he continued inclining in and lifting the motors out by hand rather than utilizing a motor crane. He was a major man and could do the undertaking easily, however, the mechanic's retailer feared the risk, so he terminated my companion.

In any case, this jobless man, with very little conventional training, took his last $200 and purchased a late-night infomercial with no cash down the land framework. In a month, he possessed his most memorable lease house.

"You want cash to bring in cash." How *genuine is that?*
Expecting that an individual is:

1. broke monetarily
2. no higher education
3. starving for essential requirements
4. deals poo house to house, strolling (couldn't manage the cost of transportation).

Presently, this individual doesn't have a lot of decisions other than asking, exchanging, and selling. Individuals will stay away from such an individual, and most treat it as an irritating subject in their life. Envision the irregular call you get from XYZ organization attempting to sell you help.

When the individual got some cash and expertise... he/she can begin assistance and carry on with work in a helpful manner.

What is the speediest method for becoming well off today?
It took Bill Entryways from Microsoft twelve years to turn into a tycoon.
It took Sergey Brin and Larry Page from Google eight years to become tycoons.
It took Jeff Bezos from Amazon four and a half years to turn into an extremely rich person.

It took Imprint Zuckerberg from Facebook four years to turn into a tycoon.

It took Jay Walker from Priceline ONE YEAR to turn into a billionaire[1].

To cut to the chase...

As you can find in the models above; "speedy" abundance isn't made straightly, yet dramatically.

Be that as it may, how would they make it happen?

They generally utilized business influence:

1. Others' time
2. Others' cash
3. Others' abilities
4. An out-of-line mechanical benefit

For what reason would destitute individuals prefer not to become rich?

Certain individuals have acknowledged their general situation and don't want more, I had an uncle that was like that. Others, I would agree most, fantasy about being rich, yet are reluctant to accomplish the work to arrive.

Then, at that point, there's the more normal methodology, those that accept cash is detestable, and the rich are eager (however it's intriguing to ask them how it was they came to be working for their boss, maybe they aren't so ravenous when a task is expected to help their loved ones). Follow all of that up with the rich need to give their reasonable part, which upon close review implies the rich ought to offer their abundance so everything is all fair (again I return to the gig thing - where will they work when the structures and hardware are completely gone for the sake of uniformity?)

How about you need to become rich?
There are a couple of justifications for why
I would avoid becoming rich:

1. Individuals would deal with me like poop because of what I have, as opposed to who I'm.

Truly, with this poo going around about "reallocating the riches", individuals would take one glance at me and generalize me with the likes of the "One Percent".

Some would dissent my actual presence, others would request a portion of my cash, others would request that I provide for good cause or strict associations "since you can, so you ought to", and citing the holy book at me ("to whom much is given, a lot is expected") to coerce me into doing anything it is they believed me should do.

Furthermore, as opposed to my personality and my activities representing me, it would be fairly how much cash I had those individuals would use to relegate "character" as far as I might be concerned, and it would constantly be a Terrible person.

Being rich all by itself implies that every other person feels like they've procured some sort of right to deal with me like poop, and that's what nobody needs.

2. I'd at absolutely no point in the future have the option to trust anybody genuinely.

Assuming I were rich, could individuals need to spend time with me since they preferred ME, or because they enjoyed that I was rich?

Besides, how is it that I could trust any heartfelt possibilities to adore me for me, and not so much for my wallet?

   3. More Cash = More Obligations = More opportunities to go to prison/get sued.

On the off chance that the total of what I have is a dollar, I should simply keep it in my pocket. In any case, if I have a huge open field of dollars, presently I need to stress over hoodlums, creatures, and unexpected whirlwinds diverting millions, I need to make a point to purchase a monster canvas before the following precipitation starts or it'll liquefy all my cash, and so forth.

My cash has turned into a living youngster that I need to safeguard and focus on.

Changes on the lookout, expansion, flattening, and so on, go about as changes in the climate and can successfully bring in my cash "debilitated" or "solid" contingent upon what's happening on the planet.

Also, I generally need to try to take it to the "Expense Specialists" for its yearly check-ups or I could be captured for carelessness.
If it breaks a window, others can "sue" for my cash to work for them in a little manner through claims.

Furthermore, if I mess up severely enough I can get shipped off prison north of a couple of bits of paper or a few lines of code because the law says I need to surrender a portion of the cash that I procured myself, to the public authority, even though said the government doesn't have anything to do with my occupation past what it self-embedded into numerous a long time before I was conceived.

4. Cash makes it more straightforward to become involved with the show.

I'm a person who trusts in holding on until union with engage in sexual relations, I'm against smoking, drinking, and taking medications. I could do without going clubbing, liking to plunk down close to a chimney and read a book, play a computer game, and so on.

Notwithstanding the way that grimy my brain can get, or how naughtily I can act, I'm one of the more held and "vanilla" individuals you could meet. I for the most part utilize web-based entertainment to vent every one of the wicked easily overlooked details I would never say or do, in actuality.

In any case, it's not difficult to be a "hero" when you don't have the means to engage in anything enticing. What, similar to I will feel terrible for not having some fat monstrous child mother like every other person?

Be that as it may, imagine a scenario in which I became rich and freely noticeable, and I can't go anyplace without a wide range of supermodels, entertainers, the Kate Beckinsale, the Elizabeth Olsens, the Jordan Carvers of the world, running out of the shadows, wet pussies abandoning a path on the, still up in the air to screw my cerebrums out before the entire world.

What do I do when my positive momentum is straightforwardly hindered by my refusal of sex, medications, liquor addiction, and general lewdness?

Might I at any point genuinely say that I have the strength of will, or of character, to decline the things I know are off-base when my constant entices me with them?

Might I at any point genuinely say I'd dare to make adversaries of really compelling individuals to make sure I can keep my feeling of pride and self-esteem?

I was unable to offer you a response until I was in that particular situation, and that alarms me.

It's not difficult to be a decent man when you're poor since you can't manage the cost of what it would cost to be anything more.

5. Crazy expansion is dangerous to my general prosperity and wanted the pattern of staying alive.

At the point when you get rich, you will have stalkers. I figure I could manage golddiggers and wannabe researchers believing I should support their cool combination projects.

However, it's the point at which we begin getting into criminally crazy stalkers that I start to have an issue, with individuals who some way or another trust that it's the fate for you to be together, have a place of worship in their storage room with each image of yours they could find, and who are continually staying nearby standing by to chloroform you and lock you in their storm cellar until you're not kidding "acknowledge their adoration" or no big deal either way.

Also, regardless of whether you figure out how to secure an adequate number of these individuals is never actually an issue, you need to manage more serious individuals who will seize you and payoff you for cash and are anticipating killing you whether or not they get their cash or not.

    6. Individuals figure they can utilize my past to denounce or potentially dishonor me.

I've composed a ton (A Ton) of shitposts in my day, some of them on this very site, as well as not having the most pleasant past in my life.

The things I've said and done, individuals I've known, and so on, can be generally found by those who decided to the point of harming me or "drop" me, dramatically overemphasizing everything, regardless of whether it happened 10, 20, or more quite a while back.

Being rich, I could do likewise to them, however at that point individuals would call me a dictator or another peevish term, since "circumstances and logical results" just apply to Others, yet never themselves. To them, there ought to never be any ramifications for what they do.
By the day's end, being rich has many advantages to the individual, their public culture, and, surprisingly, the world people, all in all, assuming that the individual is adequately rich or has the right associations.

However, the sheer measure of entanglements one can coincidentally find, the foes one can make essentially by existing, and the many different things that can turn out badly, can undoubtedly cause somebody to choose to never become well off, or if nothing else figure out how to remain inconspicuous assuming they do.

Chapter 3

Is true that you are Bound to Become Well off

What Is Your Cash Content?

I was fascinated, not such a great amount by the actual inquiry, yet rather, by the responses that others were giving.
The inquiry is: Do the most well-off 1% exercise at similar rec centers as most of us?

What amazed me was that, of the 16 responses, the majority of them said NO, the most affluent 1% Don't work out at similar rec centers as most of us.
Here is a piece from one of the solutions to give you a thought. David, who implies to be

from "The Trillionaire Examinations Division," said the accompanying:

"No. Certainly not. There are no genuine benefits to going to a public exercise center. They frequently have a crazy smell, and tacky sweat-soaked surfaces... who needs that?"

My Cash Content Response
I composed the accompanying reaction on Quora:

Indeed. The most affluent 1% (in riches, not pay) take care of business out at similar rec centers, and that is the reason they're essential for the 1%.

Much of the time, the most affluent aren't who you think they are.

Cash Content

The individual cruising all over in the huge Mercedes Benz, much of the time, is driving their vehicle on acquired cash.

The guardians who send their children to the best and most costly schools and camps are, by and large, what Stanley calls, UAWs, also called under gatherers of riches.

Some big league salary experts, who make pay rates that are in the 1% of earnings, spend their dollars on extravagance things, similar to top-of-the-line home exercise centers, vehicles, and other status merchandise, and disregard their ventures and establishing a strong financial foundation. They have enormous earnings and little riches, or as Stanley calls them, "large cap, no steers."

When something happens to the economy, their work, or their pay, they have essentially nothing to return to.

Alternately, Stanley calls the people who have enormous abundance compared with their livelihoods PAWs, also called massive collectors of riches.

You make it into the top 1% of abundance by watching your pennies, and as a shrewd individual let me know from the get-go in my functioning profession, "When you take care of your pennies, the dollars will take care of themselves."

Also, that is precisely the exact thing I did.
I saved a huge level of my business' benefits and contributed carefully. I applied the laws of compounding. I sold my business (the

one I began in 1991) in late 2017 and resigned at 49 years old.

Setting aside Cash or Saving Money

Toward the beginning of today, I worked out at the nearby $50-a-month rec center, and when I was done at the rec center, I went to the Dollar Tree Store (where each thing is $1) and purchased a couple of present packs (for an impending birthday festivity), a sack of chips, and some cleaning supplies.

Indeed. I can manage the cost of a more costly exercise center. I likewise live by the maxim that a dumb person can't help but get swindled.

Philosophical Pondering Your Cash Content

My response to this question made me contemplate my way of thinking about cash, also called my cash script.

Your cash script is your conviction about cash that is established in the manner you spend, save, and treat cash.
Your cash content will assist with characterizing your monetary result and in general monetary well-being.
For instance, if you have a couple of extra dollars, will you spend those dollars on a more costly vehicle or exercise center?

For my situation, I can bear to go to a more costly exercise center, or so far as that is concerned, I have space in excess in my home to introduce a home exercise center. I've chosen not to do all things considered. The justification for not introducing a home rec center isn't monetary, because I can prepare a home rec center very reasonably, yet more since I'm propelled by seeing others propel themselves through a portion of the very activities and loads that I do.

Then again, I struggle with paying $5 for a gift sack or card at a better quality gift shop when I can get something very similar or very much like a gift pack at the Dollar Tree Store for a negligible part of the cost. While the gift pack is a little model, a similar model can stretch out to anything, particularly vehicles and homes.

In the Quora reply, I said the accompanying: "The individual cruising all over in the enormous Mercedes Benz, as a rule, is driving their vehicle on acquired cash."

The obligation I've generally had major areas of strength for a to and that revolution has been established since youth as my granddad continually drove home the point about obligation being terrible. His convictions about obligation shaped his cash script and impacted mine. Luckily, he showed me other great cash scripts which you can learn about here: 14 Establishing long-term financial Stability Insider Facts You Want To Be Aware

I've generally seen obligation as awful. Tragically, I never truly grasped the contrast between great obligation and terrible obligation, and thusly, I didn't take a portion of the business gambles with which I might have assumed control throughout the years subsequently.

It's just over the most recent couple of years I came to comprehend that you could get cash from the bank at 5% to get a contender and make a 30% or more noteworthy return for money invested. I comprehended the idea naturally, however never remembered to try that idea.

My Three Center Cash Content Ways of Thinking

- Obligation Is Terrible:
Obligation, to me, was in every case terrible, and that was one of my essential establishing a strong financial foundation ways of thinking. It's most likely number one on my cash reasoning rundown. Whenever I've had an obligation, I've seen disposing of that obligation as a cash crisis.

I have two other center cash methods of reasoning that I've lived by for a long time.

- Cash Is the Top Dog:

I was paying attention to a webcast a day or two ago, and the host was talking about effective money management. He accepted any case from me regarding cash. He said, "Money is junk." He was rehashing an expression verbally expressed by Beam Dalio, the best mutual funds chief on the planet.

He accepts that any cash you have as an afterthought, not putting resources into the business sectors or making an arrival or some likeness thereof, is a squandered open door to procure all the more somewhere else.

I hold the contrary viewpoint, and any individual who has perused my book, The Kickass Business Person's Manual for Effective financial planning, will realize I accept that each business person ought to stand firm on an enormous foothold of their riches — a third to be exact — in fluid fixed pay bonds or money. You ought to have the option to get to that cash rapidly to make the most of chances at whatever point they could emerge.

You need to search for those valuable open doors obviously, yet assuming that you do, and the timing is correct, you should have the option to rapidly act. Furthermore, I'm not talking about purchasing a stock fundamentally, albeit that is generally a chance.

Yet, I'm talking about purchasing land, a contender, or some other venture that is simply gone marked down or where there may be a separation in the resource or resource class that you've found. Assuming that you're completely contributed, you will not have the option to make the most of those valuable open doors.

I proceed, right up 'til now, to hold a huge level of my abundance in fixed-pay ventures. You can find out about my 2019 returns and resource designation here: My 2019 Portfolio Execution and 2020 Resource Distribution Methodology.

I'm not stressed over procuring a lower return on my general portfolio. I realize I will find an open door in the following little while that will pay outsized returns, altogether higher than the couple of additional percents that I lost by not being put resources into the securities exchanges.

Also, that drives me to my last significant cash reasoning.

- *Comprehend and Play the Laws of Compounding:*

I'm certain you've heard this many times previously. Albert Einstein called building interest the eighth marvel of the world.

At the point when I allude to the "law of compounding," I'm not alluding to putting your cash in the financial exchange and procuring a compound 8% return over the long haul. Indeed, that is dependably a chance, yet the genuine abundance is made by facing determined outsized challenges and procuring a 25%, 30%, or even 35% year-on-year compound return.

How might you do that?

You can put resources into your own business. You can purchase land. You can secure a contender. What's more, the rundown goes on.

It is feasible to contribute $100,000 and emerged with $1, at least a million, in five years.

You can peruse this blog entry for instance: This is The Way to Purchase an Apartment Complex and Make an Astounding every available ounce of effort in Three Years.

I could drill down a lot more cash and establish strong financial foundation techniques. I composed this blog entry a couple of months prior: 14 Growing a substantial financial foundation Mysteries You Want to Be Aware.

The three cash methods of reasoning and my cash script aren't growing strong financial foundation methodologies. These three I recorded are my center cash ways of thinking.

What are your ways of thinking about cash? Have you posed yourself that inquiry? Do you have at least some idea what your cash script is?

Chapter 4

20 Signs You're Destined to Become a Millionaire

Start making money at a young age. Warren Buffett sold packets of gum to his neighbors at age six!

Opinions expressed by Entrepreneur contributors are their own.

Becoming a millionaire may seem like an unobtainable dream, but in reality, it's a lot more common than you think. There are 42 million millionaires worldwide in 2018, up from 36 million the year before, according to Credit Suisse's annual Global Wealth Report.

The right mentality can help you on the road to wealth. Here are 20 signs you're destined to bring in the big bucks.

- *You started making money at a young age:*

One of the most common traits that the wealthy have in common is that they began earning money at a young age. For example, 12-year-old Mark Cuban sold trash bags door-to-door, Warren Buffett sold packets of gum to his neighbors when he was just six years old and Richard Branson bred and sold parakeets as pets at the age of 11.

If you had this entrepreneurial spirit as a child, then that's a solid indicator that you've always been on the lookout for ways to make money.

- *You're an overachiever:*
Were you that student who wasn't satisfied with a B in class? Many millionaires have the mindset to shoot big. They're not satisfied with making just $1 million -- they want to make $10 million.

- *You're attractive:*
It may not be fair, but according to research conducted by Daniel Hamermesh, an economics professor at the University of Texas in Austin, "Attractive people are likely to earn an average of 3 percent to 4 percent more than a person with below-average looks." That may not sound like a fortune, but it could add up to "$230,000 more over a lifetime for the typical good-looking person." Hamermesh found that attractive

people may be better able to charm interviewers and land more sales.

- *You have an action-oriented mindset:* "Are you the kind of person who sees an opportunity and then takes action to take advantage of it? If so, congratulations, because it's that kind of action-oriented mindset that can propel you to financial freedom," writes Todd Campbell, author of Your Guide to Better Stock Picks, in a piece for The Motley Fool.

"For example, it's been proven time and time again that long-term investing can produce significantly more wealth than short-term trading, yet many Americans fail to make the most of their best long-term investment vehicle: their workplace retirement plan," Campbell continues. "Do you contribute to your workplace retirement plan? If so, do you contribute 10 percent of your income? More? Less? Considering that someone who contributes 10 percent of their $40,000 in income to a 401(k) plan at a 6 percent return has $311,572 more after 35 years than one who contributes 3 percent, under-utilizing retirement plans is a surefire way to derail you on your way to millionaire status."

● *You possess a sense of urgency:* Millionaires don't wait for the perfect time to invest or launch their business. Many of them realize that there's no better time than the present to start making money. Sitting back and waiting is one of the best ways to squash your dreams. Bottom line: Start working towards your goals right now.

- *You're focused more on earning than saving:*

It's no secret that the wealthy tend to be frugal with their money. While they excel at saving and spending wisely, they also know that one of the best ways to make more money is to invest some of what they earn.

- *You keep an open mind:*

You never know when an opportunity is going to present itself, and if you immediately shut down the thought of investing in said opportunity, then you could be losing out on making a fortune. That doesn't mean every idea is a winner -- it's important to think critically and ask the right questions before making significant moves. That's why the wealthy tend to keep an open mind when it comes to new ideas.

- *You were Mr. or Mrs. Popular in high school:*

"Moving from the 20th to 80th percentile of the high-school popularity distribution yields a 10 percent wage premium nearly 40 years later," suggests research by Gabriela Conti (University of Chicago), Gerrit Mueller (Institute of Employment Research), Andrea Gaeotti (University of Essex) and Stephen Pudney (University of Essex). In other words, if you had a significant number of friends in high school, then you may have a better chance of earning more money in your adult life.

- *You're able to live below your means:*

Another common trait that millionaires have in common is that they're usually able to live below their means. Instead of flaunting their wealth, many drive practical cars, live in modest homes, and don't spend their hard-earned cash on luxury items. (For example, my wife and I try and budget at least 50 percent of everything we make into our savings account, which we can put towards investments. These make us a lot more money in the long term.)

- *You can defer gratification:*
"Deferring gratification is one of the most important steps to becoming a millionaire," writes Jason Hall, a writer and editor for The Motley Fool. "The reality is building wealth generally takes a lot of time. Even Warren Buffett, one of the richest people alive and arguably the best investor ever,

created more than 80 percent of his vast wealth after he turned 50."

- *You have a mentor:*

It's no secret that the people you associate with can affect how successful you'll be. Think about it: If you're spending the majority of your time with people who are negative or don't have the drive to succeed, then do you think that they're going to influence you to be more motivated and optimistic?

In other words: If you want to be wealthy, start hanging out with millionaires. This won't just keep you motivated -- you also may be able to find someone willing to become your mentor and show you the ropes. If you don't personally know any millionaires, don't be afraid to reach out to them on social media or through email to start building a rapport.

- *You're not stuck in the past:*
Talking about the "good old days" may work for politicians, but it's not going to fly for millionaires. These are people who have gotten over failure, rejection, and fear, and they're most concerned with putting their energy into their futures.

- *You're a goal-setter:*
The wealthy spend time thinking about their long-term goals and needs. "You don't make a million by accident," writes Peter Voogd, founder of The Game Changers Academy, who made his first million before turning

26. "If it's not a goal, you sure as hell won't hit it."

- *You aren't divorced:*
It may seem unrelated, but according to a 2006 study out of Ohio State University, divorce could reduce a person's wealth by about 77 percent compared to that of a single person. Being married, on the other hand, maybe correlated with almost double the comparative wealth (93 percent).

"Divorce causes a decrease in wealth that is larger than just splitting a couple's assets in half," said Jay Zagorsky, author of the study and a research scientist at Ohio State University's Center for Human Resource Research. "If you want to increase your wealth, get married and stay married."

- *You know how to maximize your strengths:*
Gary Vaynerchuk once said, "I suck at 99 percent of the stuff, but I go all out on that 1 percent I'm good at."

That's not to say that you shouldn't learn something new or work on some of your weaker skills; instead, it means that millionaires can capitalize on their greatest strengths and then surround themselves with people who can enhance their weaknesses.

- *You're optimistic:*
People with the capacity to make millions don't often whine, complain or point fingers when it comes to blame. Instead, they accept

challenges and look for ways to conquer them.

"Rich people believe, 'I create my life,'" writes T. Harv Eker in his book, Secrets of the Millionaire Mindset. "Poor people believe, 'Life happens to me.'"

- *You may have a drink, but you don't smoke:*
Did you know that men who are self-reported drinkers earn 21 percent more than those who abstain from drinking, while women who drink earn 8 percent more than non-drinking females? The reason may be tied to the idea that drinking could enhance social capital, according to research published in 2006.

However, the wealthy seem to avoid smoking, according to research published in 2004. Eventually, those packs of cigarettes add up: Nonsmokers' net worth tends to be about 50 percent higher than that of light smokers and more than twice that of people who smoke heavily.

• *You have thick skin:*
Worrying about what others think of you can hold you back, so it's important to build a thicker skin. Mental toughness can lead to success since the quality can assist in handling pressure and overcoming challenges.

• *You keep up with current events:*
The most successful people in the world kick off their early mornings by catching up on

current events. For example, Warren Buffett and Bill Gates reportedly read publications like The Wall Street Journal, The New York Times, USA Today, and The Financial Times so that they can make more informed investment decisions based on what's going on in the world.

- *You're constantly improving yourself:* While having a college degree can make a difference in determining your net worth, that degree ultimately doesn't determine if you'll become a millionaire or not. Bill Gates is one of the most famous college dropouts of all time, and it hasn't stopped him from continually improving himself by reading and learning new skills.

www.ingramcontent.com/pod-product-compliance
Lightning Source LLC
Chambersburg PA
CBHW071053260726
48661CB00006B/2261